Ready to Go

Youth Group Activities

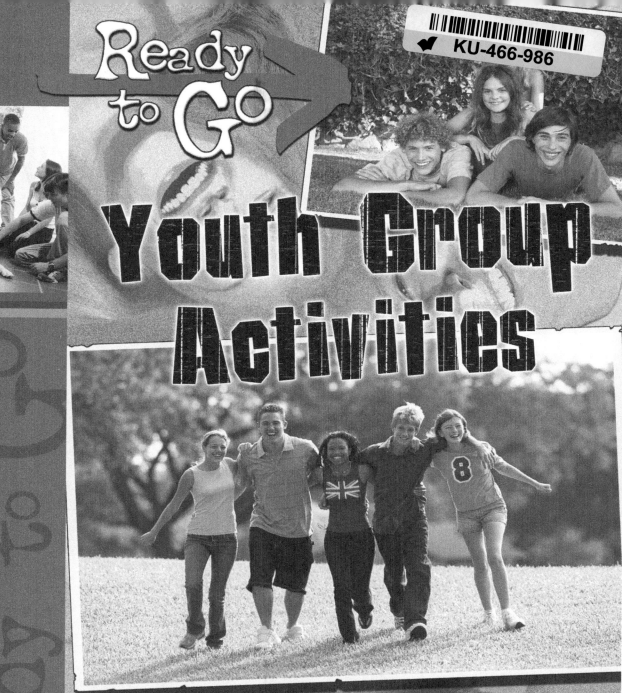

101 Games, Puzzles, & Ideas For Busy Leaders

Todd Outcalt

05 06 07 08 09 10 11 12 13 14 – 10 9 8 7 6 5 4 3 2 1

MANUFACTURED IN THE UNITED STATES OF AMERICA

Editorial Team
Editor: Jennifer A. Youngman
Production Editor: Pam Shepherd
Writer: Todd Outcalt

Design Team
Design Manager: Keely Moore
Designer: Keely Moore

COVER DESIGN: Keitha Vincent

Dedication

To the youth, staff,
and people of
Calvary United Methodist Church

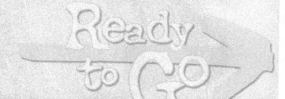

Contents

Why You Need This Book

Here's how it goes: You've planned meticulously for that youth meeting, retreat, or class—and then, inevitably, something goes awry. A featured speaker suddenly becomes sick. The teenager scheduled to lead the devotion doesn't show up. Sometimes the only thing left to do is ask a volunteer to "fill in."

In youth ministry, unexpected turns can test your nerve and summon the very best that you have to offer. And sometimes you just need that one resource to get you over the hump and transform an otherwise disastrous meeting into a top-notch event.

That's what this book is about—those last-minute, unexpected circumstances that leave you with little to no time to prepare for a youth meeting. If you've ever had to bridge the gap in an unexpected situation, you already know the value of this last-minute resource. I hope you rarely have to use it!

Ready to Go

CHAPTER 1

Ballistic Beginnings

A positive start is key to student participation in a youth group meeting. A good beginning sets everyone to moving, thinking, and learning. These activities are jump-starts that will ignite your students and set the stage for more serious quests. Some are fun, others are more cerebral—but all of these activities work well in a pinch.

1. TOOLBOX TALENTS

(1 Corinthians 12:4-6, 14-18)

Supplies: A toolbox filled with a wide assortment of tools such as screwdrivers, hammers, and wrenches. Also include some out-of-the-ordinary tools such as a tire-pressure gauge, a pair of work gloves, jumper cables, and perhaps some gardening tools or electrical tape.

Read aloud **1 Corinthians 12:4-6, 14-18**. Then say something like: "Each of us has been given gifts by God. Each of these gifts is useful and beneficial to the whole of God's work. But sometimes we need a way to discover our spiritual gifts. That's why I've brought this toolbox—as a way to help you consider your gifts. Take a few moments to look through the toolbox, then choose a tool that matches a gift or trait that you believe you possess.

"For example, you may choose a tire-pressure gauge, because you think that you are good at lifting up other people and helping to relieve the stress or pressure in their lives. Or you may choose a set of jumper cables because you believe that you are an energetic person and that your magnetism and excitement rub off on other people. Afterward be prepared to tell the group why you chose your particular tool."

Give everyone the opportunity to talk about his or her gift. This beginning can also lead to a deeper discussion of **1 Corinthians 12** or a lesson about spiritual gifts.

2. ONLY IN MY DREAMS

This discussion may generate a few laughs as well as more serious pondering about dreams and their place in our lives.

Ask the following questions and invite youth to respond by considering: What might this dream mean? What might be significant about this dream? (It surely goes without saying, but you might want to mention the difference between appropriate- and inappropriate-for-discussion dreams.)

➜ One recurring dream I have is . . .

➜ One frightening dream I have had is . . .

➜ My most vivid dream was . . .

➜ My most uplifting dream was . . .

➜ One of the things I daydream about is . . .

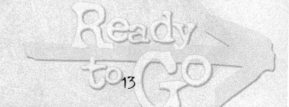

3. SHOE IN

Invite youth to gather in a circle and place their shoes in the center. Take a few moments to look over the various colors, shapes, and sizes of footwear. Spark group-building and fun by asking the following questions:

1. Who in our group has the largest shoes? the smallest?

2. Who has the most colorful shoes?

3. Who has the dirtiest shoes? the cleanest?

4. If you could trade shoes with someone in the group, who would it be? Why?

5. Who has the most unique shoes?

6. If you could walk in someone else's shoes for a day, whose would they be?

7. What do you think we can tell about other people from their shoes?

4. ARTFUL DODGERS

Supplies: An art or coffee-table book containing photographs of various paintings, sculptures, and other artwork. If your group is fairly large, you may need more than one book.

Allow the youth to look through the book and select two or three pieces of art that they particularly like or find interesting. Then ask:

1. Which pieces of art spoke most forcefully to you? Why?

2. Why do you think you were drawn to a particular painting or sculpture?

3. How can art lift our spirits?

4. How might a work of art depict spiritual themes that words might not be able to convey?

5. How does color and shape help to spark our imaginations?

6. How would you paint God?

7. How would you paint the way you feel today?

8. What colors would best describe your life right now? Why?

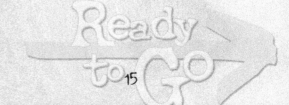

5. TABLE OF CONTENTS

If you are looking for a jump-start Bible study, ask the youth to turn to the Table of Contents in their Bibles. Ask:

1. What is your favorite book of the Bible?

2. What book of the Bible would you like to study?

3. What book of the Bible seems the most intriguing to you?

4. What book of the Bible is the most inspirational to you?

5. What book of the Bible is the most complex or difficult for you to understand?

6. With whom do you most identify in the Bible? Why?

7. What would help you to better understand the Bible?

6. CLASSIFIED INFORMATION

(Proverbs 9)

Supplies: Several pages of your local newspaper's "Classified Ads"

Give each youth a portion of the advertisements. Read aloud **Proverbs 9**, then ask the following:

1. Based upon the classified advertisements you hold in your hand, what do you think people today are seeking in life?

2. What can we learn about human need and desire from reading these ads?

3. What wisdom can we gain from thinking about our wants and needs?

4. What are some of your desires?

5. If you could write a "want ad" to God, what would it say?

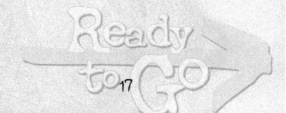

7. DYNAMIC DUOS

Divide youth into teams and compete for the best or fastest answers. Read aloud only the first half of the following famous duos (not what's in the parentheses). Add others of your own. Allow teams to identify the second half. Keep score to see which team guesses the most correct answers.

➔ Bonnie and (Clyde)

➔ Batman and (Robin)

➔ Arsenic and (lace)

➔ Fork and (spoon)

➔ Song and (dance)

➔ Peaches and (cream)

➔ Chip and (Dale)

➔ Burgers and (fries)

➔ Aquila and (Priscilla)

➔ Popeye and (Olive Oyle)

➔ Peanut butter and (jelly)

➔ Coyote and (Roadrunner)

➔ Salt and (pepper)

➔ Cats and (dogs)

➔ Hot and (cold)

➔ Jupiter and (Mars)

➔ Fish and (chips)

➔ Adam and (Eve)

8. PUNCH LINES

Begin any group session by reading aloud the following first-liners. Allow youth to complete the jokes with their original punch lines.

1. How many (blondes/brunettes/redheads/_your idea_) does it take to make soup?

2. How many (guys/girls/elephants/_your idea_) does it take to fix a car?

3. Two fleas walk into a church. One looks at the other and says:

4. Two lobsters are caught in a trap. One looks at the other and says:

5. While walking past a construction sight, two women hear a wolf whistle. One says to the other:

6. A pastor, a priest, and a rabbi are sitting next to one another at a football game. The rabbi turns to the pastor and says:

7. A squirrel and a chipmunk are fighting over the same nut. A raccoon comes along and says:

8. A funny thing happened to me on the way to the church:

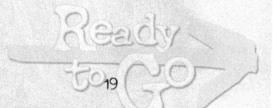

9. THE STICK-ON CLASS

Supplies: A supply of sticky notes, a markerboard or large sheet of paper, markers

Beforehand write these categories on a markerboard or large sheet of paper: *Things You Would Like to Talk About* and *Things You Can Talk About*. Post in a prominent place in the meeting room.

Hand out a supply of sticky notes, and ask youth to list five subjects each that they would like to talk about and five subjects each that they know something about (one item per sticky note). After a few minutes, ask youth to stick each sticky note under the appropriate heading on the markerboard or paper you prepared earlier.

Give the group a few minutes to prioritize each column's notes in the order they would like to talk about them.

Collect the notes and proceed to discuss the topics in the order they have been placed. If there are youth who feel confident talking about a certain subject, provide a forum for them to do so in a controlled and helpful environment. Keep the ideas for future use.

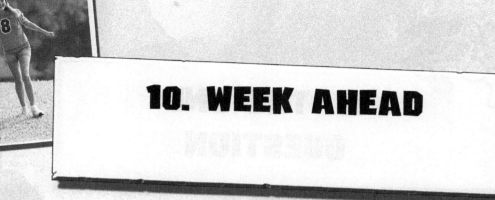

10. WEEK AHEAD

Supplies: Note cards, pencils or pens, markerboard or large sheet of paper, markers

Helping youth to think about the days ahead is an interesting way to begin a meeting. Beforehand write the phrases below on a markerboard or large sheet of paper. As youth arrive, hand out note cards and pencils, then ask each student to make notes about any decisions he or she is making that will influence the coming week. Invite volunteers to read one of their statements as a discussion starter.

In the Coming Week:

→ The biggest decision I have to make is ...

→ I am not looking forward to ...

→ I am anxious about ...

→ The one thing I hope to accomplish is ...

→ The one change I have to make is ...

→ I can always count on a good time when ...

→ The one person I need to talk to is ...

→ My biggest spiritual challenge will be ...

→ I pledge to complete ...

11. THE ONE QUESTION

This activity is not only fun but can also be insightful. Divide the group into two teams. Ask one team to complete the following statements with a question; the second team then attempts to answer the questions asked by the first team.

➜ The "One Question" I'd like to ask about love is:

➜ The "One Question" I'd like to ask God is:

➜ The "One Question" I'd like to know the answer to is:

➜ The "One Question" I'd like to ask a professor or teacher is:

➜ The "One Question" I'd like to ask our pastor is:

➜ The "One Question" I'd like to forget is:

12. HOT OR COLD

Read aloud each of the following scenarios, waiting after each for youth to tell whether they are "hot" or "cold" on the idea. For example, they either like it (and say "hot"), or they don't (and say "cold"). If time allows, ask volunteers to explain why they are hot or cold on a particular idea.

→ I would like to preach a sermon.

→ I would like to go door-to-door and tell others about our church.

→ I would like to be a high school teacher.

→ I would like to be a millionaire.

→ I would like to be poor but happy.

→ I would like to parachute out of an airplane.

→ I would like to work in a church someday.

→ I would like to be single when I am forty years old.

→ I would like to make a living with my hands (woodworking, painting, and so on).

→ I would like to work for a big company.

→ I would like to spend a summer vacation helping people in another country.

→ I would like to live to be one hundred years old.

→ I would like to drive an eighteen-wheeler for a living.

→ I would like to travel to Mars.

→ I would like to be a funeral director.

→ I would like to teach a child to read.

→ I would like to read the entire Bible.

13. YOU MIGHT BE A TEENAGER IF . . .

Invite youth to complete the following sentences.

→ You might be a teenager if . . .

→ You might be lost in your middle school if . . .

→ You might have a bad biology teacher if . . .

→ You might be eating a bad school lunch if . . .

→ You might be attending a new high school if . . .

→ You might be in trouble if . . .

→ You might be sent to detention if . . .

→ You might have too much homework if . . .

→ You might have a lousy basketball team if . . .

→ You might be in trouble if you hear the teachers saying . . .

→ You might be a recent high school graduate if . . .

→ You might be in this youth group if . . .

14. THE LONGEST PSALM (PSALM 119)

Supplies: Bibles

Hand out Bibles to students. Assign each student an eight-verse section of Psalm 119—the longest psalm in the Bible. This psalm is also an acrostic; the first line of every eight verses begins with a different letter of the Hebrew alphabet.

Ask each youth to choose and read aloud one verse from the assigned eight verses that speaks to him or her. As time allows, discuss the meaning of each verse read aloud.

15. BIBLE BOOK SCRAMBLE

Supplies: Note cards

Ahead of time, write the names of the books of the Bible on note cards (one book per card). Make two or more sets, depending upon the size of your group. Shuffle each set of cards. Divide the group into two or more teams. Give each team a set of cards. Set a time limit, and instruct each team to arrange its set of cards in the correct biblical order.

16. COLD POTATO

Supplies: Small prize, ice pack (one that is pre-packaged in a bag). If you are really short on time, you might use a small bag of ice or a large ice cube.

This exercise adds a fun twist to the old game of Hot Potato. Gather the group in a circle. Begin passing the ice pack around the circle. Whenever the leader says, "stop," the person caught holding the ice pack is "out" and must leave the circle. The last youth remaining wins a prize.

17. STORYBOARD

Supplies: Clipboard, paper, pen

Beforehand attach a piece of paper and an ink pen to a clipboard. At the top of the paper, write the sentence: *It was a dark and stormy night.*

Gather the group in a circle. Explain that you will pass around a clipboard and a piece of paper that already has one sentence written on it. Youth will use that sentence to begin a story, each person writing one sentence, adding to the story in some way, before passing the clipboard to the next person. For a large group, consider passing a second story-starter to keep the group engaged. For smaller groups, you may need to pass around the clipboard two or three times.

Once the story is complete, ask for a volunteer (or several) to read it aloud. You can also use this activity to create spiritual or personal stories. Other good beginning phrases are: *Today I was thinking about God when suddenly . . .* or *When the lights went out at church . . . .*

18. BELIEVE IT OR NOT?

Supplies: Note cards, pens or pencils

Give each youth a note card and a pencil, then ask each to write one obscure "fact" about his or her life (such as "I like spinach") and one fictional statement that might fool other group members (such as "I shook hands with a famous basketball player").

After youth are finished, invite each youth to read aloud either of his or her statements (fact or fiction). Ask the group to vote on whether they think the statement is fact or fiction. Continue until everyone has had a chance to read a fact and fiction statement. This is a great game for helping group members learn more about one another.

CHAPTER 2

Stupendous Studies

One of the most difficult last-minute youth meetings to pull off successfully is a study—whether it be a Bible study, a small-group session, or a youth-group forum on dating, for example. Here are several time-savvy studies that will help keep your pulse rate in check when you don't have the time to develop a lesson on your own. Just grab this book and lead the youth in one of these thirty-minute studies.

19. ROMANCE AND REALITY

(Song of Songs)

Supplies: Several pages of personal (dating) ads from your local newspaper

This quick-to-organize study about romance, dating, and sex is appropriate for any youth group. Give each youth a segment of personal ads. Invite the whole group to read in unison chapter 1 of the Song of Songs (sometimes called **Song of Solomon**). Then ask:

1. Based on the dating ads, what do you think people are looking for in a relationship?

2. What needs or inadequacies might be expressed in these ads?

3. Do you think it is easy to find someone to love forever? Why or why not?

4. Why do you think the Bible contains a love letter (the Song of Songs)?

5. What does this book of the Bible tell us about the need for human love and compatibility?

6. The man and woman in Song of Songs are in love. In what stage of a relationship are they? How do they express this love?

7. At what stage of a relationship do you think sexual expression should emerge? Why or why not?

8. What do you think is the Christian understanding of sexual intimacy?

9. If you were to compose a dating ad for the perfect mate, what would your ad say?

20. A TIME FOR EVERY SEASON

(Ecclesiastes 3:1-8)

Supplies: Writing paper, pencils

Begin by giving everyone a sheet of paper and a pencil. Read aloud **Ecclesiastes 3:1-8**. Ask youth to review the Scripture passage and list particular instances when they have witnessed or experienced any of the "times" mentioned in the passage (a time of weeping, laughing, gaining or losing, and so on). They may use their personal life experiences, or they may draw from observations they make about the world around them.

After a few minutes, reread **Ecclesiastes 3:1-8**, verse by verse. After each verse, invite youth to talk about the particular "times" they have witnessed. Close by asking:

➜ What do you think the writer of Ecclesiastes is trying to communicate about life?

➜ Do you think life is more heavily weighed toward the bad or the good?

➜ How might life be more "balanced" by having faith in God?

➜ How might we make the best of our own time?

➜ Do you think this view of life (the view described in Ecclesiastes) is accurate?

➜ In what ways might our feelings get in the way of our embracing a new "time" in life?

➜ In your life, which of these "times" have you experienced most often or most intensely?

Ready to Go

21. LOST AND FOUND

(Luke 15:1-10)

Supplies: Bibles, writing paper, pencils

Hand out paper and pencils. Ask youth to answer these two questions:

1. Have you ever been lost (such as in a store or in the woods)? What was it like? How did you feel?

2. Can you remember how you felt when you were found? How did this reunion take place?

Hand out Bibles. Invite one student to read aloud **Luke 15:1-10**. If you have a large group, divide students into small teams to discuss the following questions:

➡ Why do you think Jesus used stories about being lost and found to describe our need for God?

➡ What are some examples of being "lost"?

➡ Where do you see God at work in these stories? What is God doing?

➡ In what ways is God's activity related to our being "found"?

➡ What are some words that you would use to describe how God sees us?

➡ Which story speaks more to you: the parable of the shepherd and lost sheep or the parable of the woman and the lost coin? Why?

➡ How are these stories similar? How are they different?

➡ If you were telling a story about God's salvation, how would it go?

➡ Why do you think each of us needs to be "found"?

22. HERE COMES THE JUDGE!

(Judges 4:1-4, 13-24; 6:27-40; 7:16-21; 16:3-30)

Supplies: Bibles

This study focuses on the lives of three Old Testament judges: Deborah, Gideon, and Samson. Begin by forming three teams (or if you have a small group, assign one of the following passages to different youth).

→ Deborah—**Judges 4:1-4, 13-24**
→ Gideon—**Judges 6:27-40; 7:16-21**
→ Samson—**Judges 16:3-30**

Allow adequate time for the youth to read their assigned passages and prepare to retell the story for the whole group. Remaining members of the group can simply read through all the passages as they await the presentations. Then follow up with these questions:

1. How is faith in God evident in each of these judges' lives?

2. In what ways were each of these judges weak or flawed?

3. How would you describe the humanity or personality of each judge?

4. What other virtues (bravery, perseverance, and so on) are evident in each judge?

5. How was God at work through the inadequacies of each judge?

6. What might we learn about faith from these judges?

7. Why do you think God chose to work through Deborah? through Gideon? through Samson?

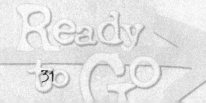

23. WHAT IS PRAYER?— PART ONE

(Psalm 6; Psalm 67; Luke 11:1-4)

Supplies: Bibles

This study on prayer includes three Bible passages: **Psalm 6; Psalm 67**; and **Luke 11:1-4**.

Divide the group into two teams and instruct each to stand in a circle. Assign each team one of the passages from Psalms. Ask the teams to read their psalms and discuss each of the following questions:

→ What emotions does the psalmist convey?
→ What heartfelt thoughts does the psalmist express?
→ What do you think the psalmist believes about life? about God?
→ What type of circumstances might the psalmist be experiencing in this text?

Allow five to ten minutes for discussion, then ask teams to briefly tell a few thoughts or feelings they discussed. Then ask:

→ What do these psalms teach us about prayer?
→ How are honesty and prayer related?
→ Do you think it is always good to share our feelings with God? Why or why not?
→ What emotions or thoughts do you have difficulty sharing with God?

Now ask a volunteer to read aloud **Luke 11:1-4**. Pause a few moments for contemplation, then ask:

→ What ideas do you think the disciples had about prayer?
→ What do you think Jesus was trying to teach the disciples about prayer?
→ What basic concepts about God does Jesus convey in this prayer?
→ What basic concepts about humanity does Jesus convey in this prayer?

Close the study with a group prayer, or invite two or three youth to offer prayers on behalf of the entire group.

24. WHAT IS PRAYER?—PART TWO

(Psalm 123; Psalm 148; Matthew 6:5-8)

Supplies: Bibles

Follow the basic format in "What Is Prayer?" (Part One). Divide youth into two teams and assign one of the following passages to each: **Psalm 123** and **Psalm 148**. Use the questions in the first study to explore the two passages in Psalms.

Then read aloud **Matthew 6:5-8** and ask:

→ Why do you think Jesus wanted to address the difficulties of prayer?

→ What dangers does Jesus talk about?

→ What basic concepts does Jesus teach about prayer?

→ What is Jesus telling us about the nature of God?

→ What is Jesus telling us about the nature or need of humanity?

→ What new insights about prayer do you derive from **Matthew 6:5-8**?

Close the study with a group prayer or by inviting the group to pray silently.

If you wish to go deeper, hand out paper and pens and invite each youth to write a three-sentence prayer. Allow those who feel comfortable to read aloud their prayers.

Ready Go

25. A STUDY IN SHEMA

(Deuteronomy 6:4-9)

Supplies: Bibles

Ask the group to read **Deuteronomy 6:4-9** in unison. Say something like: "This passage is one of the most important texts in the Bible. It helps us understand the formation of the Israelite people, as well as later traditions adopted by the Jewish faith. These traditions were certainly a part of Jesus' life, and Jesus quoted this passage on several occasions. The text is known as the Shema Prayer. *Shema* is the Hebrew word meaning 'hear' or 'listen up.' This prayer can also serve as a cornerstone for our devotion to God."

Explore the Shema Prayer in two parts. Assign verses 4–6 to one half of the group and verses 7–9 to the other half. Depending upon the size of your groups, the halves can break into smaller groups. Allow a few minutes for the groups to reread their respective passages and discuss these two questions:

➔ What do these verses tell us about God?
➔ What do these verses tell us about our human needs and relationship with God?

After groups have had adequate time to discuss the questions, call on them to explain their ideas and answers. Then ask:

➔ Why do you think this prayer is central to many people's understanding of God?
➔ Why do you think there is such an emphasis on learning and teaching?
➔ In what ways does this directive encompass every aspect of life?
➔ In what ways can we remember the presence of God without physically binding these words to our hands and homes?
➔ Why is it important for us to talk about our faith in God?
➔ How can we love God today with our whole heart, mind, and soul?
➔ If you were to choose a Bible promise as the cornerstone for your life, which promise would it be?

Close by reading the Shema, **Deuteronomy 6:4-9**, in unison.

26. STEWARDSHIP

(Matthew 25:14-30)

Ask youth to stand in a circle, then ask: "What is stewardship?" After hearing several answers, say: "A steward is someone who watches over the property or possessions of another person. According to the definition of *stewardship* in the biblical sense, we are called to be stewards over God's gifts. All that we own is a gift from God, and our stewardship is the manner in which we use these gifts."

Ask for five volunteers and assign one of the following roles to each: narrator, property owner, and three servants. Ask the narrator to read aloud the parable of the talents from **Matthew 25:14-30** while the "players" act out the passage.

After the drama, ask the following:

➜ In what ways do the inequities in this story represent life as we know it?
➜ Why do you think the property owner entrusted some servants with more and others with less?
➜ How did trust enter into the story?
➜ Why do you think the last servant hid his talent in the ground?

Now turn the talk to a more personal level. Ask:

➜ What gifts have you been given?
➜ Do you think God is entrusting you with the riches of the kingdom? How?
➜ Where do you see yourself in this story? Which servant are you?
➜ How does this story help you to see the importance of stewardship (giving God our time, talent, and treasure)?

Close with a prayer, asking God to help each person in the group to be a faithful steward of God's blessings.

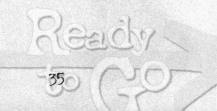

27. RICH AND POOR

(Luke 16:19-31)

Supplies: Paper, pencils, markerboard or large sheet of paper, markers

Ahead of time write the following instructions on a markerboard or large sheet of paper and post in the meeting room.

→ List three beliefs or stereotypes you think people have about poor people.
→ Now list three beliefs or stereotypes you think people have about rich people.

Hand out paper and pencils and instruct youth to make their lists following the posted instructions. After a few minutes, invite each youth to contribute one idea to the mix. Then ask:

→ Why do you think people respect rich people but rarely respect poor people?
→ Why might a person choose to be poor?
→ What dangers are there in being rich?
→ What dangers are there in being poor?

Divide youth into teams of four or five (if your class is large). Allow time for each team to read **Luke 16:19-31**. Then ask:

→ What do you think Jesus is teaching about wealth or poverty?
→ How might the condition of the human heart be affected by wealth?
→ What does this parable say about how wealth is to be used?
→ What insights do you gain from this parable about the life to come?

Close with a prayer for the rich and the poor of the world.

CHAPTER 3

Terrific Tests

Teenagers take tests all the time in school. We might even say that they are the ultimate test-takers. But tests don't have to be daunting, boring, or threatening. Here are a few fun and energetic tests that can educate, elucidate, and create last-minute excitement in your group. Answers to handout tests are provided on page 108.

28. REVELING IN RUTH

Supplies: Bibles, pens or pencils

This test focuses on the **Book of Ruth**. Allow fifteen to twenty minutes for youth to read the book. (Ruth is one of the shortest books of the Bible). Hand out copies of the test and pencils.

1. Who was Ruth's mother-in-law?

a. Oprah

b. Leah

c. Naomi

d. Orpah

2. Why did Ruth go with her mother-in-law?

a. She was bored.

b. Her husband died.

c. She was hungry.

d. It was an opportunity.

1. Where did Ruth find work?

a. Gleaning in the fields

b. At a convenience store

c. As a house servant

d. Looking after Boaz's children

4. Where had Ruth lived before?

a. Edom

b. Israel

c. Egypt

d. Moab

1. How was Boaz good to Ruth?

a. He gave her money.

b. He allowed her to glean grain.

c. He gave her a ring

d. He took her to a movie.

6. How did Boaz show honor to Ruth?

a. He invited the next-of-kin to marry her.　　b. He provided her a nice room.

c. He sent her back home.　　d. He gave her a present.

7. What deal did Boaz make with his relative?

a. He agreed to buy a donkey.　　b. He agreed to keep the faith.

c. He agreed to buy the land and marry Ruth.　　d. He agreed to visit the relative.

8. What was the sign indicating the two men had formed a deal?

a. The relative pulled out a signed contract.　　b. They shook hands.

c. They danced the hokey-pokey.　　d. They exchanged a sandal.

9. What happened after Boaz took Ruth as his wife?

a. They had a child.　　b. They obtained a quickie divorce.

c. Ruth went back to Moab.　　d. Boaz died.

10. What famous person was a descendent of Ruth?

a. Moses　　b. Abraham

c. David　　d. Sarah

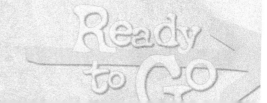

29. ACTING ON ACTS

Supplies: Bibles, pens or pencils

This "open-book" test based on the **Book of Acts** will get the group hopping. Divide youth into two or three teams and provide Bibles. Explain that the team who completes the test in the fastest time (with correct answers, of course) wins.

1. Who was elected to take Judas' place among the Twelve?

a. Bob   b. Matthias

c. Stephen   d. Archimedes

2. Who spoke to the people on the Day of Pentecost?

a. James   b. John

c. Peter   d. John Mark

1. Who was the first Christian to die for his faith?

a. Stephen   b. Peter

c. Philip   d. Martha

4. Which disciple was the first to evangelize outside of Jerusalem?

a. Mary   b. Paul

c. Larry   d. Philip

1. Who helped Saul (Paul) after he was blinded on the road to Damascus?

a. Ananias   b. Mary and Martha

c. Lydia   d. The Joppa twins

6. Who was the king who persecuted the early church?

a. Lord Vader

b. Herod

c. Caesar Augustus

d. King Henry VIII

7. Who was Paul's earliest traveling companion?

a. Barney

b. David

c. Barnabas

d. Timothy

8. What woman of Thyatira believed in Jesus and welcomed Paul and Silas into her home?

a. Martha

b. Julia

c. Rose of Sharon

d. Lydia

9. What husband and wife were leaders in the early church?

a. June and Ward Cleaver

b. Priscilla and Aquila

c. Ananias and Sapphira

d. Paul and Mary

10. What young man fell out of a window but was revived by Paul?

a. Eutychus

b. Henry

c. Demetrius

d. Aristarchus

30. THE PROBLEM WITH PAUL

How much do you know about the apostle Paul's life? Answer the following questions to test your knowledge of his life and times.

1. Paul's name was originally "Saul."   T F

2. Paul was present when Stephen was stoned to death,
and he approved of the act.   T F

3. Paul was a Sadducee.   T F

4. Paul was once shipwrecked and had to swim ashore.   T F

5. Paul was beaten and imprisoned on numerous occasions.   T F

6. Paul saw the resurrected Jesus on the road to Damascus.   T F

7. Paul was present at the birth of Jesus.   T F

8. Paul wrote many letters to churches,
and these letters are now a part of the Bible.   T F

9. Paul was a Roman citizen.   T F

10. Paul was present when Jesus was crucified.   T F

11. Paul once had an argument with Peter.   T F

12. Paul was a tent-maker.   T F

13. Paul had a mule named Festus.   T F

14. Paul was a personal friend of the Emperor Augustus.   T F

15. Paul established many new churches.   T F

31. TECHNICOLOR DREAM COAT

Take this test to learn more about the life and times of Joseph.

1. Joseph's father was Jacob. His mother was Rachel.   T F

2. We can read about Joseph in the Book of Judges.   T F

3. Joseph had many dreams.   T F

4. Joseph had a coat of many colors.   T F

5. Joseph's brothers liked him and thought he was the coolest.   T F

6. Joseph's brothers threw him into a pit
   and told their father he was dead.   T F

7. Joseph climbed out of the pit and joined the Egyptian army.   T F

8. Joseph became a trusted friend to the pharaoh of Egypt.   T F

9. Joseph eventually saved his brothers' lives.   T F

10. Joseph was the youngest of Jacob's sons.   T F

32. WOMEN OF THE BIBLE

Take this test to learn more about important women in the Bible.

1. Who was the mother of the prophet Samuel?

a. Hilda   b. Hannah

c. Heather   d. Harriet

2. Jacob worked for his future father-in-law for fourteen years and married two of his daughters. Who were these daughters?

a. Sarah and Rebecca   b. Mary and Martha

c. Leah and Rachel   d. Jennifer and Joan

1. Who found the baby Moses in the River Nile?

a. An Egyptian slave woman   b. Salome

c. A midwife   d. Pharaoh's daughter

4. David committed adultery with what woman (whom he later married)?

a. Bathsheba   b. Wanda the Gadabout

c. Hannah   d. Leah

1. What evil queen attempted to kill the prophet Elijah?

a. Queen Mary   b. Queen Leah

c. Queen Jezebel   d. Queen Latifah

6. The prophet Hosea wed a prostitute as a sign against Israel. What was her name?

a. Gomer

b. Gertrude

c. Califah

d. Jezebel

7. Who was the mother of John the Baptizer?

a. Martha

b. Mary

c. Miriam

d. Elizabeth

8. Jesus told a story about a woman who rejoiced when she found "what"?

a. A lost coin

b. A stray dog

c. A bushel basket of fish

d A new horse

9. Who was the female prophet who first spoke of the redemption Jesus came to offer?

a. Anna

b. Phanuel

c. Martha

d. Lydia

10. Who was the female judge of Israel who delivered the Israelites from their enemies?

a. Barak

b. Deborah

c. Simone

d. Sharon

Ready to Go

33. BIBLE BUILDING BLOCKS

Divide the group into two teams. Assign the following point values to each answer:

Easy questions: 1 Point
Moderate questions: 3 points
Difficult questions: 5 points

Begin by asking the easy questions, back and forth between teams. The team that earns the most points wins.

EASY

1. The mother of Jesus was _____.

2. Adam and Eve lived in the _____.

3. The first book of the Bible is _____.

4. The last book of the Bible is _____.

5. The shepherd boy who killed the giant Goliath was _____.

6. The man swallowed by a whale was _____.

MODERATE

1. She was the wife of Abraham:_____.

2. The first disciples to follow Jesus made their living as _____.

3. The first book of the New Testament is _____.

4. Moses led the Israelites out of _____.

5. Jesus grew up in the village of _____.

6. Jesus was condemned to death by which Roman governor? _____.

DIFFICULT

1. This prophet was ridiculed by a talking donkey: _____.

2. The first person to commit murder was_____.

3. The last book of the Old Testament is_____.

4. In what way was John the Baptist related to Jesus? _____.

5. Whom did Jesus raise from the dead after being
in a tomb four days? _____.

6. Where did the apostle Paul first see Jesus?_____.

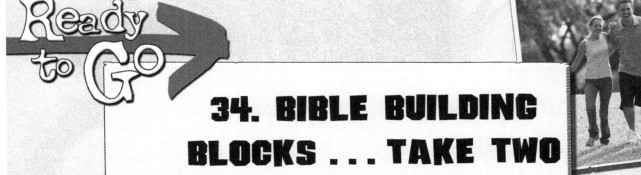

34. BIBLE BUILDING BLOCKS . . . TAKE TWO

Divide the group into two teams. Assign the following point values to each answer:

Easy questions: 1 Point
Moderate questions: 3 points
Difficult questions: 5 points

Begin by asking the easy questions, back and forth between teams. The team that earns the most points wins.

EASY

1. He led the Israelites out of Egypt: _____.

2. The Israelites crossed through the _____ to their freedom.

3. He was a strong man: _____.

4. Who said, "Love your enemies"? _____.

5. He was only a youth when God called him to be a prophet: _____.

6. He was known as Israel's wisest king: _____.

MODERATE

1. This prophet saw a giant wheel in the sky:_____.

2. He was present at the stoning of Stephen: _____.

3. She was the mother of Joseph: _____.

4. She was a judge of Israel:_____.

5. He wrote a letter to the Philippians: _____.

6. This disciple was a tax collector: _____.

DIFFICULT

1. He was the Roman Caesar when Jesus was born:_____.

2. The sons of Zebedee: _____ and _____.

3. Who said, "I will not believe unless I see the nail prints in his hands"? _____.

4. Who was the high priest of Salem? _____.

5. How many psalms are there in the Bible? _____

6. Who was the king of Israel before David? _____.

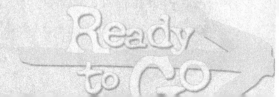

35. REMEMBER ME?

Supplies: Paper, pens or pencils

Hand out pencils and paper and tell youth to number their papers from 1 to 10. Explain that you are going to test their memories by reading aloud a story and then asking them to recall as many details as possible about the character in the story. Read the story, then ask the questions below. Keep track of who remembers the most details correctly.

Hi, my name is Amelia Vincent Roberts. People sometimes call me Bunny, but most of my closest friends call me Wiggles. I have red hair; I am sixteen years old; and I have freckles in the shape of a butterfly on my cheek. Believe it or not, I have four brothers and sisters, including a sister named Bernice, who is a constant source of irritation. She borrows my jewelry, especially my blue earrings and my silver necklace, and she makes fun of my elbows (they have pointed ends, she says). My favorite subject in school is biology, but my second favorite is literature. My locker number is 75B. In it I keep two stuffed bears and an alligator key chain. On the 26th of next month, I will celebrate my 17th birthday—then I'm going to buy a new car with blue upholstery, probably a Buick. But I'll bet you can't guess where I live.

Questions and Answers:

1. What is Bunny's second favorite subject? (*Literature*)

2. What is her nickname? (*Wiggles*)

3. What is her sister's name? (*Bernice*)

4. What does she keep in her locker? (*two bears and an alligator key chain*)

5. What is her locker number? (*75B*)

6. What day of the month was she born? (*the 26th*)

7. What make of car does she hope to buy? (*Buick*)

8. What color is the upholstery going to be? (*blue*)

9. What does she have on her cheek? (*freckles in the shape of a butterfly*)

10. What is her full name? (*Amelia Vincent Roberts*)

36. PRIVATE EYES

Supplies: Paper, pens or pencils

Hand out paper and pencils to group members. Read aloud the story, then test the group's memory by asking the questions below.

One dark and windy day, my partner Sherlock and I strode into the high school cafeteria at 3:47 P.M. The cooks were serving Ambush Stew, and two of the faucets were running. We tried to catch them, but they got away. We also realized a table was missing. It showed up later with an absentee slip from the principal. "Look," Sherlock whispered in my ear (a good place to whisper), "there's a teacher who isn't wearing any shoes. Doesn't that strike you as odd?" "Swim coach," I answered. Suddenly there was a scream. One of the students had bitten into a Jello® cube. Orange, I think, it was making quite a fuss. While we weren't looking, someone had taken a hash brown. We followed the grease trail down the hall, where it disappeared into the quarterback's locker. He's a big guy named Larry, friends call him Elmer. He wears the number 8, a senior with one eyebrow and three earlobes. Pretty fellow. However, when we opened Larry's locker, it was empty—nothing inside but a deflated football and a copy of *Sports Illustrated*. "Aha," said Sherlock, "I've solved the mystery." "What mystery?" I asked. "We're late for practice, remember?"

Questions and Answers:

1. What entrée were the cooks serving? (*Ambush Stew*)

2. Who wasn't wearing any shoes? (*the swim coach*)

3. What flavor was the Jello®? (*orange*)

4. What was the quarterback's name? (*Larry*)

5. What did his friends call him? (*Elmer*)

6. What time did the detectives enter the cafeteria? (*3:47 P.M.*)

7. What made the grease trail? (*a hash brown*)

8. How many earlobes did the quarterback have? (*three*)

9. What did they find inside the locker? (*a football and* Sports Illustrated *magazine*)

10. What was the detective's name? (*Sherlock*)

37. ODDBALLS

This test is by far the most zany. The faster you read it, the more bizarre it sounds!

On the way to Warts I met three Sorts
    who were Pudding, Dumpling, and Pie.
Said Pudding to Dumpling, "Please tell me something
    that's funny before I die."

Said Dumpling to Pudding, "You're just Hollywood-ing,
    for everyone knows you're on stage.
You only pretend to come to your end,
    so please, sir, act your age."

Then Pie follied forth, and added for worth,
    "I have a sad story to tell.
It's about three good friends who came to their ends,
    when they fell down a bottomless well."

"If it's bottomless then," said Dumpling, "my friend,
    then there's no way to sincerely know,
If they've truly expired, or just fall till they're tired,
    without sight of the bottom. You know?"

"Ah, but that is the lie," said Pudding to Pie,
  "for even the bottomless chance
To wear cleanest drawers as their mother implores,
  in case there's a hole in their pants!"

Then Pudding, he ceased, and fell from his beast,
  having laughed until he die.
And that was the end, of the three good friends:
  Pudding, Dumpling, and Pie.

Questions and Answers:

1. Who wanted to hear a funny story? (*Pudding*)

2. Who told the sad story? (*Pie*)

3. Where were the three going? (*to Warts*)

4. Who took exception to the sad story? (*Dumpling*)

5. Why was the pit not bottomless? (*Because our mothers tell us to always wear clean underwear*)

6. Who died first? (*Pudding*)

7. Who was the actor? (*Pudding*)

8. What did Pudding fall from? (*his beast*)

9. How did Pudding die? (*from laughter*)

10. What were the three friends' names? (*Pudding, Dumpling, and Pie*)

Ready to Go

38. GENESIS SCRAMBLE

Supplies: Bibles, pens or pencils

Make copies of the word scramble below. Scrambled word(s) are taken from the Book of Genesis. Give each student a copy of the word scramble and a pen or pencil.

1. AOHSN KRA

2. RABMAHA

3. RASHA

4. MADA

5. DARGNE FO NDEE

6. COAJB

7. CHRALE

8. HOAHPRA

9. PYEGT

10. AAACNN

39. DISCIPLE SCRAMBLE

(Luke 6:12-16)

Supplies: Bibles, pens or pencils

Make copies of the word scramble. Each of the words is the name of a disciple, as found in **Luke 6:12-16**. Give each student a copy of the word scramble and a pen or pencil.

1. MISNO

2. TTAMEHW

3. SMAEJ

4. WERADN

5. LIIPHP

6. THOOLMWEBRA

7. MASTOH

8. HJNO

9. SADUJ

10. TEREP

40. WHO'S WHO IN OUR GROUP?

Before the meeting, research answers to the following questions—or personalize questions to fit your group. Make copies of the quiz before answering the questions on this page (for your use as leader). Hand out copies of the quiz, along with pens or pencils. After everyone has finished, ask the questions aloud. Keep track of who answers the most questions correctly.

This person has had the most broken bones: _____.

This person has the most siblings: _____.

This person lives the farthest from the church:_____.

This person is the oldest in our group: _____.

This person has the longest scar: _____.

This person has the most pets: _____.

This person has the largest collection in our group: _____.

This person has the most fillings in his or her teeth: _____.

41. MATCH GAME

Supplies: Note cards, pens or pencils

Youth will enjoy creating this funny, fast-paced quiz. Hand out note cards and pencils or pens. Invite each youth to write one fun fact about him or herself, a strange achievement he or she may have accomplished, or a little-known personal tidbit. Remind each youth to also write his or her name on the card.

Collect the cards, shuffle them, and then read aloud, allowing time for youth to guess the identity of the person who matches each fact. Keep track of the person with the most correct guesses. This activity also makes a good ice-breaker or group-building game.

42. SPORTS BUFFS

Supplies: Note cards, pens or pencils

This energetic quiz works well with a group that enjoys all things recreational. Hand out note cards and pencils, then invite each youth to write one sports fact (a sports record, team record, or other high mark) along with the team to which it relates.

Collect and shuffle the cards. Read aloud each fact, allowing youth to guess the team related to the fact. This game also works well as a competition between small groups.

43. OPEN BIBLE

Supplies: Note cards, pens or pencils

Hand out note cards and pencils. Invite each student to think of three questions and answers about anything in the Bible and to write each question and answer on a separate note card. Collect and shuffle the cards. Divide youth into two teams and allow teams to compete for answers as you read aloud each question.

44. BIBLE BASICS

Supplies: Bibles, pens or pencils

This test is designed to stretch your group's Bible knowledge. Make copies of the test and hand out pencils or pens. Instruct youth to fill in the blanks using the correct books of the Bible. If they get stumped, they might look at the Table of Contents in their Bibles.

1. The only book of the Bible that has three k's: _____

2. A very sad book (it even sounds melancholy): _____

3. This book is sometimes referred to as "The Preacher":_____

4. The shortest name for a book of the Bible: _____

5. Royal books: _____, _____

6. The parable of the good Samaritan is found in this book: _____

7. Rhymes with "noel": _____

8. Hey, it's the title of a Beatles song: _____

9. The shortest of Paul's letters: _____

10. A queenly book:_____

11. If you like math, you'll like this book: _____

12. This book means "going out": _____

13. Lots of wisdom in this book: _____

14. The only book that sings:_____

15. There are 150 of these: _____

CHAPTER 4

Fantastic Fliers

Have you ever needed a creative poster to help advertise a youth event? Or perhaps you've wanted to design a flier to distribute at the next large youth gathering? Here are a few ideas that can spark interest (or at the very least, catch a few eyes). For maximum effect, reproduce in a larger format.

Hear Ye, Hear Ye

Let it be known throughout the _____ that the royal majesty _____ is hereby requesting the honor of your presence at _____. Each subject of the kingdom should bring _____ and should arrive promptly at _____ on the _____ in the year of our Lord, _____.

Let it also be known that any subject not appearing for this event
shall be subject to any or all of the following:

• A king's torture with thumbscrews

• A good stretching

• A fine in the sum of _____

Furthermore, be it known that any who do not appear for this event,
shall be plagued by scorpions, infested with fleas, and tormented by
assorted varieties of bed bugs.

Signed _____

PS—BYOCP (Bring Your Own Chamber Pot)

HEY, DUDE

LIKE, IT'S A REALLY GOOD TIME. SO
DON'T FORGET TO COME TO

_____

ON _____.

YOU KNOW WHAT I MEAN? REALLY
RADICAL. AND HEY, DUDE,
DON'T FORGET WHAT'S HAPPENING.
STUFF LIKE:

- _____
- _____
- _____

DUDE, LIKE THIS IS GOING TO BE WHERE
IT'S AT. YOU GET IT?
JUST BE SURE TO GET THERE, DUDE!
SEE YOU THEN.

YOUTH GROUP MEMO

Attention! Valuable spiritual training and life opportunities available. All you need is a willingness to learn. Huge eternal income available. Potential bonuses.

If you are looking to grow and learn, as well as spend time with friends, don't miss this get-together.

For more information, please come to

Event: _____

Date: _____

Time: _____

A Special Invitation

It is with great joy that the parents of
_____ request the honor of your
presence for the _____ on
_____,
to be followed by a reception at the
_____.
Please RSVP to _____.
A card has been enclosed for this purpose.

(Actually . . . my parents had nothing to do with
this invitation, and you don't have to RSVP.
By the way . . . what does RSVP stand for?
If anyone knows the answer to this one, please tell
me. And I'm not sure about the honor thing, but I
would really like to see you at the event. It would
be an honor . . . well, at least it would be a lot
more fun if you attended.

And there's not really a reception, and you don't
have to bring me a gift. I'm not really getting
married. This is just a ploy to get your attention.

MISSION IMPROBABLE

Good evening Mr./Ms. _____. By now you know of the evil plot to overthrow the world and destroy fun as we know it. Your mission (should you decide to accept it) is to attend _____ on _____ and help rid the world of this sinister madness.

Should you, or any member of your youth group be captured or discovered on the way to, or while attending, this event, your youth leader will deny having sent this information.

Please be advised that this mission is dangerous, and should you, or any member of the group, wish to turn down this assignment—well, you can't turn it down, really. Just show up! This note will self-destruct in two thousand years!

IT'S GREEK TO ME

Ουτωσ γαρ ηγαπησεν ο θεοσ τον κοσμον, ωστε τον υιον τον μονογενη εδωκεν ινα πασ ο πιστευων εισ αυτον μη αποληται αλλ εξη ζωην αιωνιον.

if this looks Greek to you . . . don't worry. Here's the scoop in plain English!

What: _____

When: _____

Where: _____

How Much $ _____

See you there!

(PS: if you want to know what the Greek says, just read John 3:16.)

IN THE BEGINNING

In the beginning,

God created _____ and said,

"Come to this event on _____,

and don't be late!"

And God saw that this event was good.

Then God said, "Let this event bring forth lots of teenagers,

and let them swarm around the fellowship hall

and creep across the floor."

And God saw that this was very good.

Then God said, "And let each teenager bring a two-liter soda

and a bag of chips, and let the food multiply over the

tops of the tables!"

And God saw that this was very good. *

*With apologies to God and the Book of Genesis.

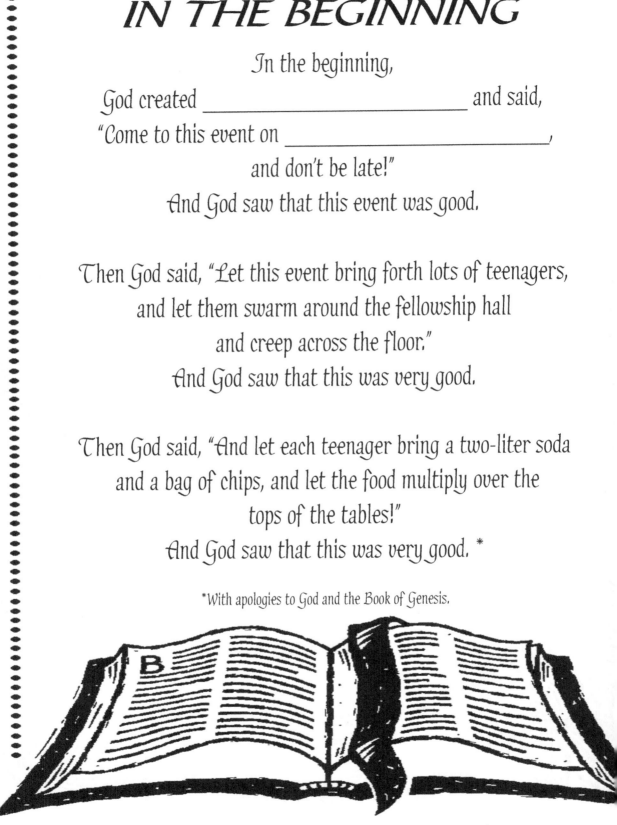

FROM THE PEN OF
WILLIAM SHAKESPEARE

Let us pluck bright honor from the nape of time

And mark our calendars now for this event:

What: _____

When: _____

Where: _____

How Much $ _____

Then let us bear with haste upon the wing

And hearken to that place that brings us all

Together in one stead—both knave and free!

Oh, that we might have some fun in this:

That saucy rascals might with one approach

To bring both something good to eat and drink—

And say, 'Methinks he doth protest too much!'

A POEM FOR YOU!

Roses are red, violets are blue,

Here is a poem just for you.

Get out your calendars, mark this down:

_____ is coming to town.

First comes the food, then comes the Bible,

you might learn something, and you're liable

to have a good time before it ends,

So be extra sure to invite your friends!

Here's the time _____, so make it snappy,

write down the place _____ and get real happy.

And don't forget to stay awhile,

Leave your frown at home . . . just bring your smile.

A DECLARATION OF FUN

Four score and seven years ago[1], most of you were not yet born. But in the course of human events, it becomes necessary to gather at

_____

on

_____

for the purpose of

_____ [2]

And, although all events are created equal, this one really stands out.[3] Plan to attend, so that a youth group of the youth, by the youth, and for the youth shall not perish from the church.[4]

[1] *We think this is a fancy way of saying "eighty-seven"*

[2] *Here are the details:*

_____

_____

[3] *How, you say? Here are more details:*

_____

_____

[4] *OK, so the group is not going to perish, but we'd really miss you if you weren't there!*

LISTEN UP!

I'M ONLY GONNA SAY THIS ONCE.
YOU SAVVY? YOU DON'T GET IT,
THEN I SEND IN THE GOONS—
JUST A LITTLE HEAT TO HELP YOU
MAKE UP YOUR MIND!

SO HERE'S THE DEAL. I'M MAKIN'
YOU AN OFFER YOU CAN'T REFUSE.
YOU SAVVY?
IT'S THE BIG

_____

AND IT'S HAPPENING ON

_____

YOU DON'T SHOW, THEN WE GOT A
PROBLEM. THE BOSS DON'T LIKE IT.
THEN BOBO HAS TO COME OVER
TO HELP YOU FIND YOUR WAY TO

_____

YOU KNOW WHAT I'M SAYIN'?

SO DON'T MAKE ME DO IT. GET
THIS ON YOUR CALENDAR. TATTOO
IT ON YOUR ARM IF YOU HAVE TO.
IF BOBO AIN'T HAPPY, AIN'T
NOBODY HAPPY. YOU SAVVY?

PS: THIS AIN'T A BLACK-TIE AFFAIR, PUNK.
JUST COME AS YOU ARE.

CHAPTER 5

Prodigious Parables

Religious teaching is often illustrated by narrative and story. Jesus himself used parables to speak of spiritual matters and to offer insights into the kingdom of God as well as human relationships. Toward that end, here are several lessons based upon biblical parables, creative narratives, and other teaching stories—all designed to help youth discover new truths about God and one another.

56. FIT TO BE KING

(2 Samuel 11:1-21; 12:1-15)

Supplies: Bibles

Gather youth in a circle and ask them to consider unspoken responses to these questions:

→ Have you ever acted inappropriately? How?
→ What happened when you were confronted with your wrongdoing? How did you respond?

Invite the youth to read **2 Samuel 11:1-21**. Then ask:

→ What sin did David commit?
→ How did David attempt to cover up his sin?
→ How did David's actions grow worse as he tried to conceal what he had done?
→ How might David's actions be typical of our human response when we have done wrong?

Next, invite the youth to read the parable, along with David's response, found in **2 Samuel 12:1-15**. Say something like: "God sent a prophet named Nathan to speak to David. Nathan told David a parable. Let's see how this parable helped David to understand the depth of his mistakes as well as David's response."

After reading the parable, ask:

→ How did the prophet's parable relate to David's situation?
→ Why do you think the prophet used the imagery of rich and poor?
→ How did David initially interpret this story?
→ How did David come to understand the story after being confronted with his sin?
→ How did David respond to the prophet's words, "You are the man!"
→ How might the parable have saved David from a worse fate?
→ What can we learn from David's story, or this parable?

57. A FARMER'S STORY

(Matthew 13:1-9)

Supplies: A supply of small seed packets, Bibles

If possible, plan to meet outdoors and choose a spot that offers several topographical features, including hard or rocky ground (or concrete or asphalt), good ground, and a place where weeds are already growing. Beforehand obtain some small seed packets.

Invite someone to cast the seeds across the ground (using a sweeping motion of the hand as the seeds are released). After the seeds have been scattered over the ground, ask the following questions:

→ Which of these seeds do you think has the best chance of growing into maturity? Why?
→ Which of these seeds might begin to grow but not reach maturity? Why?
→ What are some of the soil characteristics, or ground features, that can play a significant role in the growth or detriment of these seeds?
→ What other ingredients would be important to the seeds' growth?

Read aloud **Matthew 13:1-9**, then ask:

→ Why do you think Jesus used seeds to illustrate God's kingdom?
→ What do you think Jesus is saying about our lives?
→ What are the important ingredients in the growth of our faith?
→ What are some characteristics that can "choke" our faith or "strangle" our enthusiasm for God?
→ What can we add to our lives that will strengthen our faith?
→ What might be some "weeds" that we need to clear out of our lives?
→ What do you think would be representative of the "harvest" in this parable? What are we trying to accomplish as Jesus' followers?

Ready to Go

58. TELLING THE STORY

Supplies: Paper, pens or pencils

Invite youth to use the following elements and characters to create a parable. Or, divide the group into smaller groups or teams and ask each to develop a compelling story that illustrates some point of faith.

Allow youth to choose one of the following settings:

→ A desert

→ A mountain top

→ A deep chasm and a bridge

Suggest they choose one or more of the following people to include in the parable:

→ An old man or an old woman

→ A lost child

→ A wise man or a fool

→ A priest or an unbeliever

Assign youth one of the following questions to illustrate:

→ What is faith like?

→ What is God like?

→ What is love like?

Invite each small group or team to read aloud or act out its parable. As time allows, discuss the parables and learn how other youth feel about the stories by asking:

→ How did this parable speak to you?

→ What insights did you gain from this parable?

59. GOOD SAM

(Luke 10:30-37)

Supplies: Bibles

The parable of the good Samaritan provides the basis for this quick in-depth discussion. Hand out Bibles and invite youth to read the story individually or in small groups. Then ask:

→ Why do you think the first two people (priest and Levite) passed by the man in need?

→ Who might these people represent today?

→ How might we see ourselves in these people?

→ Why do you think the Samaritan stopped to help?

→ What point was Jesus trying to make by using a Samaritan as the helpful one?

→ Who might the innkeeper represent in this parable?

→ In what ways is the innkeeper important to the outcome of the story?

→ As disciples of Jesus, how is our faith tested each day when we see others in need?

→ In what role do you see yourself in this parable (priest, Levite, Samaritan, innkeeper, injured person)?

→ Based on this parable, what does it mean to be a "good neighbor" or a "good Samaritan"?

60. GUIDELINES FOR LIVING

Use the following parables to help teenagers apply biblical principles in their lives. Read aloud each story, then ask the youth to tell how they would respond in each instance, and why.

→ Once there were two friends who had never had an argument. One day the first friend asked the other, "How do arguments begin?" The other friend placed a rock between them and then said: "See that rock. I say I want it. Then you say 'I want it.' And we have an argument." So the first friend said, "The rock is mine." The second answered, "No, it's mine!" "You're right," said the first, "it's your rock. You take it!"

→ There was a woman whose only son died. After some weeks, when she could not shake her grief, she went to see a wise man. The man said: "I know a remedy for sorrow. Find a mustard seed from a home that has known no sorrow, and you will be free of your grief." So the woman went from house to house looking for people who had never known heartache. She found none. But each day, as she visited from house to house, her grief lessened.

Questions:

→ What does this story teach?
→ What lessons can we learn from this story?
→ What biblical principles might apply to the parable?

76

61. THE SILVER WINDOW

This parable is about wealth and the dangers of greed. Tell or read aloud the story, then discuss the follow-up questions.

Once there was a man who lived in a home high atop a hill overlooking a village. Each day, the man looked out of his window and watched his neighbors, often praying for those he noticed in the valley below.

One day, however, the man learned that he had inherited a sizeable sum of money. Immediately he thought of his neighbors and all the help he could provide. But he also said to himself: "How beautiful my window would look if I could adorn the edges of it with silver. Surely a little silver would not hurt."

So the man used some of his wealth to adorn the edges of his window. Each morning, when he looked out of his window, he watched his neighbors in the valley below. But he also enjoyed the window itself. And there were times when he wondered how beautiful the window might be if he added even more silver.

As time went by, the man added more and more silver to the window. Finally, one day when he looked out, he could not see his neighbors anymore. All he could see was his own reflection.

Questions:

→ Do you think wealth changes people? Why or why not?
→ In the beginning of this story, what did the man regard as his life purpose?
→ How did this purpose change?
→ What do you think this parable teaches?
→ What is the significance of the silver window?
→ How did the window reflect the man's changing attitudes and values?
→ What other choices could the man have made with his money?
→ How might a different decision have helped the man?

Ready to Go

62. SEVEN FISH

Read aloud the parable, then discuss the follow-up questions.

Once there was a man who had a wife and five children. Every morning he went to the river to fish, and every day he caught seven fish—one fish for every member of his family. The man was happy, and he always said, "God will provide." But there were times when he thought, "If only I could catch an extra fish, I'd have more for myself." But no matter how hard the man tried, he could never catch an eighth fish. In time, however, his desire for an extra fish consumed his thoughts.

One evening as the man was preparing to go to bed, he learned that one of his children had been killed in a tragic accident. The man was heartbroken, but when he awoke the next morning, he thought: *Finally, today I will have an extra fish, for I always catch seven.* That day, however, he caught only six fish. And no matter how hard he tried, he could not catch a seventh.

Questions:

→ What do you think this parable teaches about God's provision?
→ What might have caused the father to think he needed an extra fish?
→ How is this parable similar to our modern-day attitude toward consumption and obtaining "things"?
→ What does this parable teach about life?
→ What does this parable teach about greed?
→ How does the idea of God's provision return at the end of the story?
→ Do you think this parable rings true to life? What would you add to the message?

63. SHORT STUFF

Supplies: Note cards, pens or pencils

Divide the group into teams of three to four. Assign teams one parable each and instruct them to read the parables and determine what truths the parables teach. Hand out note cards and pencils for teams to use as they process their thoughts and record ideas. After a few minutes, ask teams to explain what they think their parables teach.

1. There were two sisters. One was thin and beautiful, and the other was heavy but very intelligent. When she was young, the thin, beautiful sister was loved by many, but as she grew older, her beauty faded and she became deeply depressed. The other sister, however, became more beautiful as she grew older, but she refused to love. One day the younger sister remarked to the older, "If only we could trade places, because we each have gained what the other lacked."

2. Once there was a woman who had never owned a mirror. Someone asked her, "If you have never seen your own reflection, then how do you know what you look like?" She replied: "I do not have to see myself to know that I am beautiful, nor do I need a mirror to see and know who I am on the inside."

3. Twin brothers were separated at birth. One went east, and the other went west. They spent their lifetimes looking for each other. When they were very old, they accidentally encountered each other on the street. One said, "If I didn't know any better, I'd say that you look like the brother I have been trying to find my entire life." The other replied, "I too have been looking for my brother, but I have found him a thousand times before."

4. A man owned a valuable ring. While fishing in a lake, he lost the ring. A fish swallowed it. Then a heron swallowed the fish. Finally, the man shot the heron. He took it home, cut it open, and discovered his lost ring. He said to himself, "God has now taught me the most valuable lesson of all."

64. THE HIDDEN TREASURE

Read aloud the following parable, the ask the follow-up questions.

One day a man was working in his field when a prophet appeared to him. The prophet said: "Soon you will come into a lot of money. You may use this wealth for seven years, but afterward, I will return and take back the money. So be sure to use it wisely."

As soon as the prophet disappeared into heaven, the man ran home to tell his wife the good news. On his way there, he tripped over a stump, fell into a hole, and discovered a hidden treasure. The man took the treasure to his house and told his wife how he had found the money and what the prophet had said.

For the next seven years, the couple used the money as wisely as they could. When the time had passed, the prophet returned to claim the money. "Where is the money God gave you seven years ago?" the prophet asked. "I have come to claim it."

"It is not here," said the woman. "We gave it away."

"And who has it now?" asked the prophet. "For I must return it to God."

The man opened his window and pointed to his neighbors' homes. "We have used the money wisely," he said. "We gave money to one person to pay for an operation. To another we gave money to care for a sick child. And to another we gave money to build a home."

One by one, the man related the ways they had used the money. The prophet smiled. "Indeed, you have lived well," said the prophet. "Therefore, you shall receive even greater blessings from God."

➜ What do you think is the truth of this parable?
➜ What surprises did you discover in this parable?
➜ In what ways did the couple use the money wisely?
➜ What lessons might we learn from this story?
➜ If you could summarize this parable in one sentence, what would it be?

65. A JAR OF MEAL

This short parable will get your teens thinking about the kingdom of God and prompt discussion of the following questions: *What is the kingdom? How do we make it known?*

A woman set out on a journey. To prepare for it, she loaded a jar with grain and slung it over her back. However, she could not see that there was a small crack in the jar. As she walked along the path, the grain slowly leaked out. Finally, when she arrived at her destination, she was surprised to see that the jar was empty. This is what the kingdom of God is like.

→ What might the jar in this story represent?

→ What might the journey represent?

→ Why was the woman surprised at the end of her journey?

→ Was the empty jar, in your opinion, a good thing or a bad thing?

→ How does this parable give insight into the kingdom of God?

Ready to Go

66. MUSTARD SEED FAITH

(Luke 13:18-19)

Supplies: A mustard seed

If possible, bring a mustard seed to show during this lesson. Begin by asking the youth:

➜ What is the smallest object you have ever held in your hand?

➜ What is the largest tree you have ever seen?

➜ What is your favorite bird?

Next, invite one student to read aloud **Luke 13:18-19.** Then ask:

➜ What do you think Jesus was teaching about the kingdom?

➜ Why do you think Jesus used the example of something tiny growing into something large?

➜ What is the significance of the birds in this story?

➜ How is the concept of growth important to our faith?

➜ How is the concept of growth important to our understanding of the kingdom of God?

➜ What modern-day examples of this same lesson can you think of?

67. LAMPS AND LIGHTS

(Luke 11:33-36)

Supplies: A flashlight

Begin this lesson by turning out the lights in the meeting space, then ask the following questions (using a flashlight if necessary).

→ What would it be like to sit in darkness for a long time?

→ What emotions do you experience when forced to sit in darkness?

→ What do you think it would be like to be blind?

→ How would you describe darkness to another person?

After turning on the lights, ask:

→ Why is light valuable to us as human beings?

→ What emotions do you attach to being in the light?

→ How would you describe light to another person?

Next read aloud **Luke 11:33-36**, then ask:

→ What points do you think Jesus was trying to make with this parable?

→ How are light and darkness symbolic of the human condition?

→ What might light and darkness represent in human life?

→ How would you retell this parable to another person?

68. TV PARABLES

Most youth have one or two favorite television shows that they watch regularly. Use this activity to help youth think about the lessons that can sometimes be learned from television shows. Form small groups or teams and hand out copies of the following questions. Encourage students to talk freely about any lessons they have learned from a favorite show.

1. What is your favorite television show? Why?

2. Who are the main characters on this show? Describe their personalities.

3. How does this show speak to real-life issues? What are they?

4. Can you think of a particular episode that taught you a lesson? What was it?

5. If you could write a script for a television show, what would it involve?

6. Which character on the show do you most identify with and why?

7. Can you think of any lessons you've learned that you have applied to your life? What are they?

69. NATURAL PARABLES

Plan to meet outdoors for this lesson. Choose a rugged area—the more rugged, the better. To begin, invite each youth to roam the area (provide a specific time frame and a firm return time) in search of an object that can be used to tell a story or parable. Ask each youth to think of creative ways he or she might weave the object into a parable about life, faith, or spirituality. A few examples follow:

→ A rock can be used to tell a story about standing firm or having a solid foundation.

→ A flower can be used to weave a parable about love or about seeing beauty in unfamiliar or unexpected places.

→ An ant might be the perfect illustration to use in talking about persistence, resiliency, or taking on difficult or overwhelming tasks.

When all of the youth have returned from the nature search, sit in a circle and encourage each one to relate his or her story using the chosen object.

Ready to Go

70. DINNERTIME

(Luke 14:12-24)

Supplies: A variety of snacks (such as small sandwiches, donuts, fruit, cookies)

Beforehand arrange a table with the snacks you prepared. As the youth gather to eat, ask:

→ How do you feel when you are invited to a fancy dinner?

→ Who, do you think, is normally invited to a banquet?

Read aloud the parable of the banquet in **Luke 14:12-24**. Then ask:

→ Why do you think Jesus used the banquet setting to teach about the kingdom of God?

→ Why do you think people refuse God's invitations?

→ What makes the guest list in the parable insightful?

→ What does this story say about God?

→ Who might be included in God's guest list today (in our world)?

→ Where do you see yourself in this parable?

CHAPTER 6

Radical Recreation

This chapter provides exciting games that can be organized with minimum effort. Some ideas teach; others are just plain fun—but all of these activities will get youth moving and thinking.

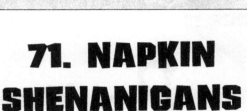

71. NAPKIN SHENANIGANS

Supplies: A package of paper napkins

Invite the youth to fold the paper napkins to make animals, figures, or geometrical shapes. This is a good activity to use prior to a dinner party, allowing the napkins to be used at the table or as party favors. If you want to step it up a notch, use linen instead of paper napkins and see who can come up with the most creative design or shape.

72. CAPTURE THE FLAG

Supplies: Two flags, note cards, pens or pencils

This game works best in a large area such as a fellowship hall or a gymnasium. Divide youth into two teams—as if you were going to play an actual game of Capture the Flag. However, instead of looking for the flags, with students running hither and yon, each team will compile a list of ten clues that will reveal the position of its flag to the opposing team.

Hand out note cards and allow time for teams to write their clues on individual note cards, numbering each from 1 to 10. To begin, invite each team to hide its flag (as in the actual game), then read aloud one of its clues to the other team. Each team then gets one chance to guess where the flag is hidden. A wrong guess results in a team having to "give up" one player to the other team. The winner is the first team (still intact) to guess the correct location of the other team's flag.

73. MAKE-UP ARTISTS

Supplies: Face paints or theatrical paints, clean-up supplies

Although messy, this game is loads of fun. Divide youth into two or more teams, and give each team a supply of face paint. Each team chooses one individual to act as its "model," and the other team members do their best to "make up" this person in a certain way. Options include: the prettiest, most horrifying (always popular!), or the funniest.

74. ICE-CUBE CAPERS

Supplies: Refrigerator ice cubes, small cooler

Just fill a small cooler and let the games begin. Game options include:

→ See who can pick up an ice cube using only the tongue (the drier the ice, the better).

→ See who can melt an ice cube the fastest by pressing it between their palms or holding it under an armpit. A wilder option is to divide youth into teams and have some team members pressing the ice cubes to other team members' backs.

→ Play any version of an "ice-cube relay" that suits your fancy: Blow the ice cubes across a tabletop or tile floor using straws. Toss the cubes from person to person, or pass them around a circle. Any relay that keeps the ice moving will work.

→ See who can create ice-cube figures by melting the ice in the form of animals, shapes, and so on.

Ready to Go

75. MOSAIC MAYHEM

Supplies: Assorted mosaic tiles, glue, sheets of sturdy cardboard or wood

Get those artistic juices flowing by allowing youth to create their own works of art by gluing the mosaics to cardboard or wood. Consider choosing a group theme for the pieces of art, perhaps a biblical theme or one that reflects the spirit of your youth group.

76. REALITY SHOW NIGHT

Supplies: Markerboard or large sheet of paper, markers, writing paper, pens or pencils, props

Invite students to create a reality show using this quick improvisational idea. Divide youth into teams. Ask each team to perform a specific task or develop a specific event, drawing ideas from some of the more popular reality shows that teenagers enjoy, such as *Survivor*, *Fear Factor*, *The Amazing Race*, and *Big Brother*. Display a list of these shows (and other appropriate shows) to generate creativity and ideas for this fun event.

77. HIDE THE EYEBALL

Supplies: A rubber eyeball

Check out the local dollar store and purchase a rubber eyeball. You'll be surprised at how much fun you can have hiding the eyeball around the meeting room. Divide youth into two teams. Have one team leave the room while the other team hides the eyeball. When the first team returns to the room, it must locate the eyeball. Then reverse the fun.

78. BOOK SCAVENGER HUNT

Supplies: Copies of the books used to compile the scavenger list, pens or pencils

Consider playing this game in a church library. Beforehand compile and duplicate a scavenger hunt list that includes words, phrases, or character names that youth must locate by looking in specific books. Here are a few examples:

→ What is the first word on page 100 of our copy of *War and Peace*?

→ What is the central character in the book *(insert the title of a book that you used to compile your scavenger list)*?

→ What is the last word of the Bible?

Hand out the scavenger lists and pencils, and announce a time limit. When time is up, check to see which individual (or team) located the most correct answers.

Ready to Go

79. LOCK BOX

(1 Samuel 16:6-13)

Supplies: A lock box, small safe, or other storage container, note cards, pens or pencils

Lock Box is a fun addition to an indoor gathering. Bring along a lock box, small safe, or other storage container from your home (cleaning out only those "valuables" or contents that you might consider too personal for youth to see). Also, if you like, include a few fun items that the youth might not expect to find.

Gather youth in a circle, setting the box in the center. Hand out pencils and note cards and invite students to list five items each they think are inside the lock box. Allow about five minutes for students to work, then reveal the box contents.

This activity may also be used to lead a discussion or biblical lesson on the topic of judging people on the basis of their insides rather than what we see on the outside. **Use 1 Samuel 16:6-13** as a biblical reference.

80. POPSICLE™ OLYMPICS

Supplies: A large box of Popsicles™

Looking for a cool summer game? Purchase large boxes of Popsicles™ for the group. Then organize one or more of the following games as a recreational treat.

1. See who can eat a Popsicle™ the fastest (without biting it!)

2. See who can remove the Popsicle™ from the stick without breaking the ice.

3. Divide youth into teams and see which team can create the first wooden teepee using the Popsicle™ sticks.

92

81. WHAT'S IN YOUR WALLET?

Supplies: Your wallet—filled with items similar to those listed below

This game yields fantastic fun. Beforehand place some odd items in your wallet to assure a few laughs. These fun items might include: a membership card to the Mickey Mouse Club (or some other strange organization); a picture of your spouse after you've blacked out his or her eyes; a phony bill for some absurd item; a high school prom picture; belly-button lint; a picture of an old boyfriend or girlfriend; your driver's license (especially if you have a funny mug shot); a punch card to a fictional restaurant.

Ask youth to sit in a circle. Invite each student to name one thing he or she believes is in the your wallet.

82. SITCOMS

Supplies: Note cards, pens or pencils

Hand out note cards as youth enter the meeting room. Invite them to list names of characters from television sitcoms (one per card—character name only and not the name of the sitcom). Collect the cards (the more the better) and divide the group into two or more teams. Give each team several cards. Establish a time limit (ten minutes works well) and tell each team to identify the matching sitcom for each character. The team with the most correct matches wins.

Ready to Go

83. LINE KICKBALL

Supplies: A ball of any size or shape

This game requires plenty of running, teamwork, and energy. Choose an open grassy area in which to play. Picture the playing field as a large rectangle, with the shorter ends as "bases"—two lines extending from sideline to sideline. One team lines up behind the first baseline and takes turns kicking the ball into the playing field occupied by the other team. A ball kicked outside the boundaries is an out. A ball caught in the air is an out. When a player kicks the ball, he or she must run to the other "base" at the far end of the field without getting hit by the ball thrown by an opposing player. Teams score a run for each person who is able to run from one end of the field to the other without getting hit by the ball.

84. CLUES TO THE KINGDOM

(Matthew 5:3-10)

Supplies: Slips of paper, plastic Easter eggs, colored markers

This game is appropriate to play at Easter. Prepare two sets of slips of paper, eight slips of paper in each set and each set written in a different color. Each set should contain one Beatitude per card, as found in **Matthew 5:3-10**. Beforehand place each card inside a plastic Easter egg and hide the eggs outside.

To play, divide the youth into two teams. The first team to find a complete set of "Beatitude eggs" wins. Follow up with a discussion of these teachings and encourage youth to follow Jesus' instructions as a way of discovering the kingdom of God.

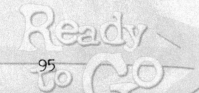

85. ARMPIT RELAY

Supplies: A large ball

This game is fun to watch, difficult to complete, and requires a very large ball. Divide youth into two teams and ask each team to form a line. The goal is to pass the ball as quickly as possible from person to person. But there's one important rule: The ball must be passed from armpit to armpit; no other parts of the body may help in the transfer (especially the hands).

86. TOILET-PAPER HATS

Supplies: Several rolls of sturdy toilet paper

Divide youth into teams and provide several rolls of sturdy toilet paper to each. The winner is the team who creates the most unique, the most beautiful, the funniest, or the tallest toilet-paper hat.

87. BODY PAINTING

Supplies: Several different colors of body paints, small prize

For only a few dollars, you can purchase body paint in several different colors. Use the paint and these ideas to turn a last-minute rush into a fun event.

→ Pair off youth and have each person create a unique design on the back of his or her partner's hands.

→ Assign a number to each color of body paint that is available. Have youth roll up their sleeves and create designs on their arms. Encourage them to draw the outlines of images that will require the use of several different colors. When designs are complete, youth should write the assigned number for each necessary color in the appropriate space of the picture. Then pair up youth and allow them to complete the paint-by-number designs on their partners' arms. Give a small prize to the pair who finishes first.

88. PUTTIN' ON THE RITZ

Supplies: A woman's blouse (preferable with small buttons), skirt, necklace, hat, gloves, hose, and so on in as large a size as possible, an open-top cardboard box a pair of dice

This game can be played indoors or out. Beforehand assemble an entire women's outfit using the items listed above. Store the outfit in an open-top cardboard box. Play the game as follows:

→ Sit in a circle. Position the box of clothing in the middle of the circle. Pass the dice clockwise around the circle, allowing youth to take turns rolling the dice.

→ When someone rolls a 7, that person must immediately stand up, run to the box, and try to completely dress (over their clothes) in the wardrobe ensemble before another person can roll a 7.

→ If another person rolls a 7 before the first person can complete the ensemble (which is usually the case), that person begins taking clothing from the first person and trying to dress in the ensemble as well.

→ When someone rolls an 11, the first person who began dressing in the circle must remove any clothing and sit down.

→ The game continues until someone completes the ensemble, wearing all of the articles of clothing.

YOUTH GROUP ACTIVITIES

89. GARDEN OF WEEDIN'

If your church has a good size lawn or if you are located near a park or field, try this quick outdoor game in the spring or summer. Set a time limit, then allow youth to pick as many dandelions as possible in the allotted time. Whoever has picked the most dandelions at the end of that time is the winner. This race provides fun for the youth, and your church's lawn and garden crew will appreciate the help in eliminating these pesky, but pretty, weeds.

90. FAR OUT

Supplies: A Frisbee™, a soccer ball, or a softball

Mark a boundary in your available space. Invite each teen to hurl, kick, and throw each object as far as possible. Keep a record of the accumulative distance for all three activities and calculate a winner. If your group is competitive, divide youth into teams and calculate a team winner.

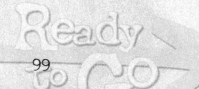

91. HIDE THE (YOUR SILLY OBJECT) HERE

Supplies: stuffed animal or plastic cartoon figure

Choose a silly stuffed animal or plastic cartoon figure to be your group's mascot. First hide the toy in a fairly conspicuous location, then get more creative in your hideouts. After a while, tell the youth that the first person to see it gets to hide it somewhere else.

If you preach on Sunday mornings, it's fun to hide it in a place that youth will see while you're preaching.

CHAPTER 7

Enlightening Endings

A good conclusion to a youth meeting accomplishes several purposes: It leaves the youth wanting more; it offers an invitation to return; and it refreshes the spirit. This chapter offers a dozen enduring and endearing endings that will motivate youth as they grow.

92. THANK-YOU NOTES

Supplies: Stationery or cards, pens or pencils, names and addresses

Make someone's day and enlist youth to write thank-you notes. Provide a supply of stationery or cards, as well as the names and addresses of people in your congregation who deserve special recognition or thanks. Possible recipients are the members of your choir or band and those who serve as teachers, ushers, or greeters. Also consider writing thank-you notes to those whom your youth identify as unsung heroes of the congregation—people who work hard but do not receive recognition for their efforts or ministries.

93. CARE PACKAGES

Supplies: Shoeboxes, hard candies, hot chocolate mixes, bookmarks, stationery, and refrigerator magnets

Enlist youth to assemble care packages for shut-ins, college students, or church members (or their family members) serving in the military. Work with your church secretary or pastor to compile names and addresses.

Allow youth to choose the items for their boxes, but encourage a variety of items. Also create name tags with your youth group's name printed on them to attach to the refrigerator magnets. Assembling these care packages is one way your teens can make a difference to others as well as raise individual awareness of their servant roles.

94. CANDLELIGHT PRAYERS

Supplies: Candles, candleholders, matches

Candlelight prayers are a meaningful way to close a youth meeting. Beforehand position several candles in what will be the center of your group. Then gather youth in a circle (around the candles), light several of the candles (leaving a few for youth to light), and turn out the room lights. Allow students to light the unlit candles for people they know who need special prayers. As you go around the circle and more candles are lit, the room will begin to glow, creating an atmosphere for prayers to be offered silently or aloud.

95. AFFIRMATION SENTENCES

Gather youth in a circle and invite them to take turns completing the following sentences:

→ One thing I learned today was: _____.

→ Someone who really encourages me is:_____.

→ I'm happier today because:_____.

→ I'm a better person today because of: _____.

Ready to Go

96. BUILD-ME-UPS

Ask youth to stand in a circle, then ask for one volunteer to stand in the middle. The person in the middle walks slowly around the interior of the circle, then shakes hands with one person in the group. As the middle person shakes the other person's hand, he or she says that person's name, then offers two affirmations that begin with the first letter of that person's name. (Some examples are: "Tonya, I think you're terrific and thorough." "Bob, I think you're brave and bookish.") The person who has been affirmed then responds by saying the name of the person in the middle, offers two affirmations that begin with the first letter of that person's name, and then replaces the middle person in the circle. Repeat the process until everyone has been the middle person at least once.

97. LET IT OUT!

Gather youth in a circle and invite them to take turns responding to the following affirmation prayers, completing the sentences as they feel led.

→ One thing I need from God is: _____.

→ I'm truly thankful for: _____.

→ Our youth group is special because: _____.

→ I would like to pray for: _____.

YOUTH GROUP ACTIVITIE

98. POETRY CORNER

Do you have a favorite poem? Are there students in your group who like to read or write poetry? Bring a poem to read aloud, or invite youth to bring and read some of their originals. Reading aloud poetry can prompt a meaningful closing moment. Remember to include time for reflection and comment.

99. BAG OF IDEAS

Supplies: A large bag (a cloth bag works best), note cards, pens or pencils, markerboard or large sheet of paper, markers

Sometimes the best idea is a "wild idea" from your youth. Use this activity to create a "thoughtful" conclusion to a youth group meeting. Beforehand list the following categories on a markerboard or large sheet of paper and display in the meeting space: (1) Recreation, (2) Learning, (3) Opportunities, (4) Outings, (5) Service, and (6) Worship.

As youth arrive, hand out note cards and pencils. Invite youth to list ideas for activities to use in youth group meetings. Explain that they should think in terms of the categories listed on the chart you prepared earlier. After a few minutes, collect the note cards and place in the bag. If you have time, discuss some of the ideas. Keep the bag handy and use the ideas as needed and at appropriate times.

Ready to Go

100. ANGELS ON EARTH

Supplies: Note cards, pens or pencils, bulletin board or large sheet of posterboard, glue or tape, markers

Hand out note cards and pencils. Invite the youth to write the names of people they would consider to be "angels on earth"—people who have made a difference in others' lives. Use the cards to design a bulletin board by the same title. Another idea is for youth to write and mail thank-you notes to the "angels."

101. BE-ATTITUDES

(Matthew 5:3-11)

Gather youth in a circle and read aloud **Matthew 5:3-11**. Ask students to adopt a "be-attitude" that they will commit to living out in the coming week. Go around the circle and ask each youth to express his or her reasons for selecting the particular "be-attitude." For example, one teen might express a desire to be more "poor in spirit" or humble. Another teen might express a desire to be more meek, or to become a peacemaker at school. After everyone in the circle has participated, re-read the Scripture passage.

Ready to Go

Answers to Terrific Tests

28. Reveling in Ruth: 1-c; 2-b; 3-a; 4-d; 5-b; 6-a; 7-c; 8-d; 9-a; 10-c.

29. Acting on Acts: 1–b (Acts 1:16); 2–c (Acts 2:14); 3–a (Acts 7:59-60); 4–d (Acts 8:26, 40); 5–a (Acts 9:10-17); 6–b (Acts 12:1); 7–c (Acts 12:25); 8–d (Acts 16:14-15); 9–b (Acts 18:18, 26); 10–a (Acts 20:9-12).

30. The Problem With Paul: 1–T (Acts 9:1); 2–T (Acts 7:54-8:1); 3–F (Philippians 3:5); 4–T (Acts 27:39-44); 5–T (Acts 28:17-31); 6–T (Acts 9:1-9); 7–F; 8–T; 9–T (Acts 22:28-29); 10–F; 11–T (Galatians 2:11-14); 12–T (Acts 18:3); 13–F; 14–F; 15–T.

31. Technicolor Dream Coat: 1–T (Genesis 30:25); 2–F; 3–T (Genesis 37:5, 9); 4–F (Genesis 37:3); 5–F (Genesis 37:4); 6–T (Genesis 37:23-33); 7–F (Genesis 39:1); 8–T (Genesis 41:37-40); 9–T (Genesis 45); 10–F (Genesis 42:34).

32. Women of the Bible: 1–b; 2–c; 3–d; 4–a; 5–c; 6–a; 7–d; 8–a; 9–a; 10–b.

33. Bible Building Blocks: *Easy:* 1–Mary; 2–Garden of Eden; 3–Genesis; 4–Revelation; 5–David; 6–Jonah; *Moderate:* 1–Sarah; 2–Fishermen; 3–Matthew; 4–Egypt; 5–Nazareth; 6–Pontius Pilate; *Difficult:* 1–Balaam; 2–Cain; 3–Malachi; 4–Cousin; 5–Lazarus; 6–Road to Damascus.

34. Bible Building Blocks . . . Take Two: *Easy:* 1–Moses; 2–Red Sea; 3–Samson; 4–Jesus; 5–Jeremiah; 6–Solomon; *Moderate:* 1–Ezekiel; 2–Paul; 3–Rachel; 4–Deborah; 5–Paul; 6–Matthew; *Difficult:* 1–Augustus; 2–James and John; 3–Thomas; 4–Melchizedek; 5–150; 6–Saul.

38. Genesis Scramble: 1–Noah's ark; 2–Abraham; 3–Sarah; 4–Adam; 5–Garden of Eden; 6–Jacob; 7–Rachel; 8–Pharaoh; 9–Egypt; 10–Canaan.

39. Disciple Scramble: 1–Simon; 2–Matthew; 3–James; 4–Andrew; 5–Philip; 6–Bartholomew; 7–Thomas; 8–John; 9–Judas; 10–Peter.

44. Bible Basics: 1–Habakkuk; 2–Lamentations; 3–Ecclesiastes; 4–Job; 5–1 Kings, 2 King 6–Luke; 7–Joel; 8–Jude; 9–Philemon; 10–Esther; 11–Numbers; 12–Exodus; 13–Proverbs; 14–Song of Solomon; 15–Psalms.

YOUTH GROUP ACTIVITIES

Scripture & Theme Indexes

Some of the activities in this book have a direct link to a Scripture or theme. Where possible, we've indexed the activities for you. We hope you find what you're looking for and that you'll be "Ready-to-Go" at your next gathering!

Ready to Go

Scripture Index

("A" refers to the activity number where that Scripture is used.
"P" refers to the page number.)

YOUTH GROUP ACTIVITIES

12:1	A29, P41	
12:25	A29, P41	
16:14-15	A29, P41	
18:3	A30, P42	
18:18, 26	A29, P41	
20:9-12	A29, P41	
22:28-29	A30, P42	
27:39-44	A30, P42	
28:17-31	A30, P42	

1 CORINTHIANS

12:4-6, 14-18	A1, P12
13	A103, P108

GALATIANS

2:11-14	A30, P42
5:22-23	A102, P108

PHILIPPIANS

3:5	A30, P42

Theme Index

Note: Not all of the activities in this book fall into theme categories, however, those listed on these pages are fairly obvious.

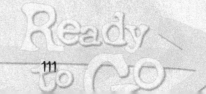

YOUTH GROUP ACTIVITIE

Lightning Source UK Ltd.
Milton Keynes UK
UKOW061918150713

213847UK00009B/571/P